WHAT IF?

WHAT IF?

✦

...a reflection on hair

by
Samia Boctor

Illustrations
by
Robert Gilliam

iUniverse, Inc.

on hair

DEDICATION

To my beautiful daughters, sons and
children. This book is for you as you
inspiration and motivation.

To my wonderful husband for his supp
and technical expertise.

To all of us who fuss or fussed abou
hair....

What if we all had
the same exact hair
and hair style?

How would it be?

uld it be very short?

Short?

Shoulder length?

Mid-back length?

Very long?

Or, perhaps,
NO hair at all?

Would the hair be
very curly?

Slightly curly?

Wavy?

Straight?

Or in dreads?

ld the color be black?

Dark brown?

Medium brown?

Light brown?

Red?

Blond?

Grey?

Or even pink?
Blue?
Green?
Purple?
Or Rainbow?

Would we keep
the hair in braids?

A pony tail?

Pig tails?

A bun?

just hanging down?

Would we all look
exactly the same
from the outside?

Would you like tha

Why?

at about our real self

we think, feel and act)?

Would we all then
be the same
because our hair
is the same?

es our hair change

our real self?

Can you tell how
the real person
is from looking
at their hair?

hy do some people
 a really difficult time
hen they don't like
eir hair sometimes?

Does this change

who they really are

hy do some people
make fun of
ther people's hair?
w do you think they
feel?

What do you thin
of your own hair?

it were a different
texture,

length, or color,

f you have no hair at
all,

would this change

who you really are?

Everyone has differe

answers to these quest

and they are all tru

for you at this tim

you meet different
people
ith varieties of hair,
ne back to this book
and
er the questions again.
ı just might find out
that you'll have
ferent answers every
time.

Now, what if
I tell you
a little secret?

You are

so beautiful

and handsome

exactly as you are!

Your inner beauty sh
like a radiant light fo
the world to see.

THE END